40 DAYS OF WORSHIP

A Devotional Guide to a Deeper Connection with God

40 Days of Worship

A Devotional Guide to a Deeper Connection with God

Theresa Murata

40 Days of Worship: A Devotional Guide to a Deeper Connection with God
By Theresa Murata

A portion of this text has been compiled from the book *Dancing With Silks: Moving with the Wind of the Spirit* and formatted as a daily devotional.

ISBN 978-0-9909789-1-6

Published by:
Worship Expressions
PO Box 106
Elmhurst, IL 60126-0106
www.worshipexpressions.net
Printed in the United States of America

Cover design by Pixel Studio
Author photo by Julie Riley

For ordering information contact:
Worship Expressions
www.worshipexpressions.net
worshipexpressionsmin@gmail.com

ACKNOWLEDGEMENTS

Thank you, Diane Belz, for the opportunity you gave me to teach and mentor students in worship dance and the Word of God. My time as an instructor at the Upper Room Dance Studio was an inspiration for this book.

Special thanks to Lisanne Kaufmann for your editing, and to Lynn Peterson, Karen Smith and Susan Solar for your feedback on the manuscript. I truly value your friendship, encouragement, and heart of integrity for the Lord and His Word.

INTRODUCTION

You are about to embark on an exciting and beautiful journey.

Do you have a desire to fulfill God's call for your life? Do you want to hear God's voice with greater clarity? Do you want to experience a deeper, more intimate connection with God? Worship is a key to all these things and so much more.

Over the next forty days, we will be exploring various aspects of worship. The heart of worship involves cultivating an intimate relationship with God. God desires for us to know Him more than merely on an intellectual level; He wants us to experience Him.

For the Word of God to take root in our heart, we not only need to hear it, but we must also understand and apply it (Matthew 13:19-23, James 1:22-25). This book is designed not only to bring a deeper understanding of worship, but also as a practical guide to apply revelation from the Word in a way that invites an increased engagement with God and a deeper connection with Him.

The **Activation** section of each day's reading is intended to activate and awaken your spiritual senses to connect with God in a deeper way. Each **Activation** consists of a practical exercise to help you apply the Word of God in a way that facilitates experiencing more of Him in your life. In the beginning, you may find it challenging to quiet your heart and mind from distracting thoughts. Or you may feel awkward doing some of the exercises, as the ideas may be new to you. Don't give up! With practice and a willingness to try new things, it will become easier. Soon you will develop a lifestyle of going deeper with God and drawing new strength from your relationship with Him.

To get the most out of the *40 Days of Worship* experience, it is recommended that you set aside some time in a quiet, comfortable place where you can focus on the Lord without distractions. Then invite the Holy Spirit to come and speak to your heart. Take a deep breath, relax, and enjoy your journey deeper into the heart of God. He is waiting for you!

DAY 1

Romans 12:1 (ESV) – I appeal to you therefore, brothers, by the mercies of God, to present your bodies as a living sacrifice, holy and acceptable to God, which is your spiritual worship.

What is true worship? According to Romans 12:1, our spiritual worship involves presenting ourselves to God as a living sacrifice. It has been said that the problem with a living sacrifice is that it keeps crawling off the altar! So worship is a daily lifestyle of yielding ourselves to God. In Romans 12:1, when Paul states that he is appealing to us "by the mercies of God," he is drawing our attention to the goodness and love of God. In other words, our response to God's goodness and love is to present ourselves to Him as a living sacrifice. As we grow in our revelation of God's love and goodness, our natural response will be to worship Him. Worship is an attitude of our heart, submitted to God, and in constant awareness of His love for us.

Activation:
Lie down in a quiet, comfortable place on the floor or bed. If it is not possible to lie down, this activation may also be done seated in a comfortable position. Close your eyes and picture yourself lying on an altar. It is the altar of God's love. Enter into a place of resting in God's love and yield your heart to Him. Picture presenting yourself to God as a living sacrifice and let Him consume you with His love.

Psalm 100:4 – *Enter into His gates with thanksgiving, and into His courts with praise. Be thankful to Him, and bless His name.*

There is a difference between *praise* and *worship*. Giving praise to God is good and necessary! We enter the courts and gates of God through thanksgiving and praise. Praise and thanksgiving are powerful weapons that can literally change the atmosphere around us and bring us out of worldly mind-sets into the heavenly courts of God.

However, *worship* is where we enter into the Holy of Holies. Worship is the place of intimate, face-to-face encounter with God. Worship is where we enter into the secret place and connect with God's heart. It is a place of rest and abiding. Worship is a place of intimacy with God, which is God's intention for us. That is why He sent His Son Jesus, so we could experience intimacy and union with Him. There is strength in our intimacy and union with the Lord, which is so needed for the days to come. There is a lot going on in the world, and we need to learn how to access our secret place and draw strength and wisdom from our union with the Lord.

Activation:
Write down at least ten things you are thankful for, and at least ten attributes of God for which to praise Him. Then speak your thanks and praise out loud to God. See yourself entering His gates as you thank Him and His courts as you praise Him.

DAY 3

1 John 4:19 – *We love Him because He first loved us.*

Worship is our response to God's love for us. It is our heart's natural response to receiving a revelation of God's love.

When I was in Bible college, our director said something that has stayed with me. She told us to take a little time each day to let God love us. During this time, we were not to tell God how much we love Him or even praise or thank Him, but just to focus on letting God love us and receiving His love. At first, it was hard for me to not start praising God and thanking Him but to just rest and receive His love. But as I began to practice doing this, I realized how much God enjoys loving on His children. Have you ever held a baby in your arms and just delighted in holding, looking at, and loving him or her? The baby did not have to say or do anything. It was just delightful to hold and love on the child. Oftentimes I feel like we do not give God enough opportunities just to hold and love us.

Psalm 46:10 – *Be still, and know that I am God.*

Sometimes it is good just to be still and let God hold us in His arms and love on us. As our Heavenly Father, He delights in His children.

Activation:
Sit in a comfortable position and close your eyes. Let your heart become quiet and enter into a place of rest. Feel the tension leaving every muscle of your body as you enter into relaxation. Feel the gentle arms of your loving Heavenly Father holding you. His heart delights in you. He is so pleased with you. Just rest and receive His love.

1 Corinthians 1:9 – *God is faithful, by whom you were called into the fellowship of His Son, Jesus Christ our Lord.*

Have you ever asked God, "What is your call on my life?" God has a divine purpose and destiny for each of our lives and it is important to find out what it is. Walking in God's plan for our life will not only bring fulfillment and satisfaction to us, but it will also abundantly bless others. Although God has a unique plan for each of our lives, we all have a higher calling.

A number of years ago, I was worshiping at a women's meeting and I heard the Lord say, "Your highest calling is to worship Me." Regardless of what else God has called us to do, our highest calling is to worship at the feet of the King. It is a place of rest.

We are called into fellowship with Jesus Christ our Lord, and worship is a place where we experience intimate communion with our God.

Activation:
Set aside some time to play some worship music. Pick at least one or two songs, preferably with lyrics that describe who God is. Close your eyes and think about these characteristics of God. Feel your heart connecting with Him in fellowship and communion.

DAY 4

If you feel led to, you may also want to take communion, in remembrance of what Jesus has done for us. As you receive the elements, representing His body and blood, feel the bread and wine/juice becoming a part of your body and meditate on the intimate fellowship we have with Jesus. He is a part of us, and we are a part of His body (John 6:48-58, 1 Corinthians 11:23-34).

* * *

DAY 5

> John 4:23-24 – *The hour is coming, and now is,*
> *when the true worshipers will worship the Father in*
> *spirit and truth; for the Father is seeking such to*
> *worship Him. God is Spirit, and those who worship*
> *Him must worship in spirit and truth.*

The primary difference between worship in the Old and New
Testaments is that in the New Testament, worship is much
more personal. In the Old Testament, the Holy Spirit came
upon certain people to accomplish a specific purpose.
However, in the New Testament, because of what Jesus
accomplished on the cross for us by paying the price for our
sin and making us righteous and holy, the Holy Spirit is able to
actually dwell on the inside of us! We no longer have to worry
about the Holy Spirit leaving us. Once He comes inside us,
He's here to stay! So when we worship God, it becomes very
personal because God's Spirit is actually inside us!

So, how do we worship? We worship in spirit and truth.

To worship God in Spirit is about connecting spirit to Spirit. It
is not just going through the external motions of worship but
getting our heart involved and connected with God. To
worship in truth, we need to know Who we are worshiping.
Jesus Himself declared in John 14:6 that He is "the way, the
truth, and the life." To worship in truth, we need to know the
Living Word of Truth (John 1:14, Hebrews 4:12).

Activation:
Read John 1:14 and Hebrews 4:12. Spend some time
meditating on these verses and letting Jesus, the Living Word,
speak to your heart.

DAY 6

1 Thessalonians 5:23 – Now may the God of peace Himself sanctify you completely; and may your whole spirit, soul, and body be preserved blameless at the coming of our Lord Jesus Christ.

Worship is one of the most powerful activities we can participate in. Of course, the Word of God is also very important and powerful. However, the Word by itself without a relationship with God becomes law. Worship is where we enter into a relationship with the Living Word.

We are a three-part being—spirit, soul, and body. As born-again believers, our spirit is already in perfect union with God (1 Corinthians 6:17). But in worship, we willingly yield our soul (mind, will, and emotions) and body to God.

Worship is where we bring every area of our lives into subjection to the Lord (Romans 12:1-2). In worship, we are aligning our whole selves—spirit, soul, and body—with the Word of God. This is probably why we see a lot of healing and deliverance happen during worship. I have been at many conferences where the Spirit of God begins to move on people during worship and people receive physical or emotional healing. I have personally experienced deliverance during worship. I have a friend who is a worshiper. One time he had gotten poison ivy and it was not getting better. Then he heard God tell him to take out his guitar and start worshiping Him. As my friend worshiped the Lord, the poison ivy disappeared!

DAY 6

Activation:
Find a comfortable place to sit or lie down. Set aside some time, at least five-ten minutes, or more if possible. Play some worship music, either with or without lyrics. Close your eyes and picture yourself—spirit, soul, and body—coming into alignment with God and His Word. Feel yourself joyfully and willingly yielding your soul (mind, will, and emotions) and body to God.

* * *

2 Corinthians 3:18 – *We all, with unveiled face,
beholding as in a mirror the glory of the Lord, are
being transformed into the same image from glory
to glory, just as by the Spirit of the Lord.*

Another powerful thing that happens during worship is that we
become like the One we behold.

As we spend time in worship beholding His face, we begin to
reflect His image and His glory. Exodus 34 describes how
Moses' face shone with the glory of the Lord whenever he met
with the Lord face-to-face. People will notice when you have
been in the presence of the Lord. There have been times when
I have experienced a special time with the Lord and people
have remarked about the peace or joy they felt around me. But
it is much more than an outward manifestation. When we
spend time face-to-face with God, our heart also begins to
reflect His heart, and our character, His character. Reflecting
the image of God is just a natural by-product of spending time
with the Lord.

Activation:
Find a comfortable place to sit or lie down. Choose at least one
or two worship songs that help you put your focus on the Lord.
While the music is playing, close your eyes and picture
yourself face-to-face with God, gazing into His eyes, and
reflecting on who He is.

Matthew 6:9-10 – *In this manner, therefore, pray:*

> *Our Father in heaven,*
> *Hallowed be Your name.*
> *Your kingdom come.*
> *Your will be done*
> *On earth as it is in heaven.*

Jesus taught us to pray to our Heavenly Father, inviting His kingdom to come and His will to be done on earth as it is in heaven.

Worship brings the atmosphere of heaven to earth. We literally change the atmosphere as we worship. It was previously mentioned that we often see healings happen during worship. Why does this happen? It is because we are bringing heaven to earth. There is no sickness in heaven; therefore heaven is manifesting on earth during worship, and sickness has to leave. What is heaven like? In heaven, there is no lack, all wisdom and knowledge is available, and there is an atmosphere of peace and joy. Heaven has the solution to every problem.

Worship opens a realm of access to heaven's resources. In worship, our hearts and minds come into alignment with heaven's perspective and it enables us to effectively release heaven's purposes on earth. God's will be done on earth as it is in heaven!

DAY 8

Activation:
Spend some time reflecting on what heaven is like (Revelation 7:16-17, 21:1-7, 22:1-5). Then pray, "On earth as it is in heaven!" As it is in heaven, so let it be on earth! You are God's agent to bring forth heaven's purposes on earth. Declare out loud: "I am God's agent to bring forth heaven's purposes on earth!"

* * *

DAY 9

Psalm 34:3 – Oh, magnify the LORD with me, and let us exalt His name together.

In worship, we concentrate our focus on the Lord. Sometimes we become so focused on the problem that we cannot see the solution. Whatever we focus on is what becomes magnified in our field of vision. For example, if I put my hand directly in front of my face and stare at it, my hand becomes the biggest thing I see in my field of vision. However, if I take my focus off of my hand and look beyond it, I see a much bigger picture. In worship, we fix our eyes on the Lord so that the solution can come into view.

I used to wonder what it meant to magnify the Lord. If God is already big, how do we magnify Him? We magnify Him by setting our focus on Him. He is the solution to our every need.

Activation:
Find a comfortable place to sit or lie down. Choose a few worship songs that help put your focus on the Lord. It may be helpful to find songs with lyrics that focus on who God is, but any song that helps bring your focus to the Lord is fine, with or without lyrics.

As the music plays, close your eyes and practice focusing on the Lord. Keep looking to Him until He fills your vision. Enjoy being in this place with Him. The Lord has become bigger than any problem you face. Remember what it feels like to magnify the Lord—when He becomes bigger than anything else in your field of vision. You can come back to this place in your mind and heart anytime.

DAY 10

Song of Solomon 7:10 – *I am my beloved's, and his desire is toward me.*

Worship is where we experience intimacy with the Lord. We were all created with a need for intimacy. This need was first and foremost designed to be met by God. In the Garden of Eden before the fall of man, Adam and Eve experienced perfect union with God. In fact, they were so God-conscious that it did not even occur to them that they were naked (Genesis 2:25). God is the only one who can perfectly meet our need for intimacy. He meets that need as we spend time with Him in worship.

We belong to God. He is our Beloved, the lover of our soul, and His desire is toward us. The word "desire" implies a strong longing for. The strong longing of God's heart is for us to intimately know Him.

Being born again without enjoying worship is kind of like getting married and never enjoying an intimate relationship with your spouse. How many people have said a prayer to ask Jesus to come into their life but not really experienced God beyond that? God loves us and desires us to know Him intimately in a relationship. As we experience His love and goodness in this relationship, our natural response will be a desire to serve. Serving God does not replace knowing Him. A life of true worship and service flows out of an intimate relationship with God.

DAY 10

Activation:
Set aside some time today to focus on the Lord. It may be going for a walk and thanking Him for the beauty of creation. It may be sitting quietly and listening to the birds singing, and meditating on how God takes care of us (Matthew 6:26). Or it may be listening to a song that helps you focus on who God is and His love for you. Enjoy His company, and feel your heart connecting with His. Sharing and enjoying intimate moments with the Lord helps build intimacy in our relationship with Him.

* * *

DAY 11

John 3:16 (ESV) – *God so loved the world, that he gave his only Son, that whoever believes in him should not perish but have eternal life.*

God has called us to experience intimate relationship with Him. That was His whole purpose in sending Jesus.

John 3:16 is probably a familiar verse and many people believe that "eternal life" means that we will live forever in heaven if we put our trust in Jesus. While this is true, there is so much more being communicated in the words "eternal life." In fact, Jesus Himself defines "eternal life" for us in John 17:3:

John 17:3 – *This is eternal life, **that they may know You**, the only true God, and Jesus Christ whom You have sent.* [emphasis mine]

Jesus defines "eternal life" as knowing God. This is not just a casual knowing about God. The Greek word "know" is *ginōskō*, which means "to know by observation and experience. To be involved in an intimate, growing relationship." This same word is used to convey the thought of connection or union, as between a man and woman. This is a very intimate kind of knowing. And this is the kind of intimacy God desires to have with us.

God wants us to experience him intimately, and that happens in worship.

DAY 11

Activation:
Sit in a quiet, comfortable place with a journal or notebook and a pen. Focus on the Lord and His love for you. If you were the only person on earth, He would have come to rescue you. He loves you with an everlasting love.

In your journal, write the questions, "God, why do You love me? How much do You love me?" Then take a deep breath, relax and listen to the still, small voice in your heart, and write down what you hear. If you are having difficulty hearing at first, it may be helpful to begin by writing "My child...," and then listen for the response to fill in.

[Note: When journaling, if you feel distracting thoughts or "to-do list items" coming to your mind, write them down on a separate piece of paper to address later. Then relax and bring your focus back to the Lord.]

* * *

DAY 12

John 15:5 – I am the vine, you are the branches. He who abides in Me, and I in him, bears much fruit; for without Me you can do nothing.

Jesus invites us to abide in Him. Abiding in Him is a place of intimacy.

Why is intimacy with God important? First of all, without intimacy, nothing would be birthed. Things are birthed through intimacy and relationship. If our parents did not have an intimate relationship with each other, we would not have been born. Things in the Spirit realm are also birthed through intimacy and relationship. Jesus taught that the Word of God is a seed (Matthew 13). When we meditate on the Word of God, the seed of the Word gets planted in our spiritual womb. Worship is the place where we experience intimate relationship with the Living Word. Many of the things that I have seen God manifest in my life were conceived in the place of worship. Worship is the place where things of the Spirit are conceived in us and in time, birthed through us.

Activation:
Sit in a quiet, comfortable place with a journal or notebook and a pen. Focus on the Lord and His presence. Picture yourself abiding in Him. Rest in His love. You are in a safe place.

In your journal, write the question, "Lord, what do You want to tell me today?" Take a deep breath, quiet your heart, and listen for His still, small voice in your heart. Write down what you hear. If you are having difficulty hearing at first, it may be helpful to begin by writing "My child…," and then listen for the response to fill in.

DAY 13

John 10:27 – My sheep hear My voice, and I know them, and they follow Me.

In John 10, Jesus tells us He is the Good Shepherd who gives His life for the sheep. He assures us that His sheep hear His voice.

Intimacy is important because that is where God shares His heart with us. Worship fine-tunes our ability to hear God's voice. God is always speaking to us, but many times we are too preoccupied with our own thoughts and activities to hear what God is saying. In worship, we quiet our minds and focus on God and learn to listen to what He is saying. When we set our full attention on Him, our ability to hear Him improves. For example, when I worship on the violin, I often begin to enter into a time of prayer or intercession. When I worship, I am connecting with God's heart and He begins to share things with me that He wants to pray through me.

Activation:
Sit in a quiet, comfortable place with a journal or notebook and a pen. Focus on Jesus, the Good Shepherd. Say out loud, "Jesus, You are my Shepherd, and I am one of Your sheep. Therefore, I hear Your voice, and I follow You."

In your journal, write the question, "Lord, what do You want to tell me today?" Take a deep breath, quiet your heart, and listen for His still, small voice in your heart. Write down what you hear. If you are having difficulty hearing at first, it may be helpful to begin by writing "My child...," and then listen for the response to fill in.

DAY 14

Psalm 91:1 – *He who dwells in the secret place of the Most High shall abide under the shadow of the Almighty.*

We were made to live out of our intimacy with God. This is our "secret place." It is a place of peace, safety, and protection.

To "dwell" means "to make one's home; reside; live." To dwell somewhere means to make one's residence there. It is not just a temporary place we visit. To dwell in the secret place of the Most High means not just spending a few minutes with God and then going about the rest of the day without thinking about Him, but rather remaining in awareness of the presence of God, moment by moment. Our life was designed to flow out of our relationship with God. This is the heart of worship.

Activation:
Sit or lie down in a comfortable place and let your heart become quiet before God and enter into a place of rest. Picture yourself entering into a face-to-face union with God. It may be helpful to play some soft worship music that facilitates directing your focus on the Lord, or to visualize a beautiful place, such as a garden. Spend some time resting in His presence.

This is your secret place with God. It may take some practice at first, but the more you practice the easier it becomes to enter into your secret place.

2 Chronicles 20:21-22 – *When he had consulted with the people, he appointed those who should sing to the LORD, and who should praise the beauty of holiness, as they went out before the army and were saying:*

> *"Praise the LORD,*
> *For His mercy endures forever."*

Now when they began to sing and to praise, the LORD set ambushes against the people of Ammon, Moab, and Mount Seir, who had come against Judah; and they were defeated.

A few years ago, the Lord spoke to me, "Worship is our warfare." True worship is supernatural activity. When we praise and worship the Lord, corresponding activity is happening in the spirit realm.

If I were a military strategist, I would probably think of sending the most well-trained and best-equipped warriors at the head of the army. The Lord's strategy was to put the worshipers at the head of the army to declare His praises. As the worshipers began to sing and praise the Lord, He set ambushes against Judah's enemies, and their enemies were defeated.

The battle is the Lord's but we participate with Him through praise and worship. Our part is to praise the Lord, and the Lord will deliver us and give us the victory.

Day 15

Activation:
Praise generally involves some sort of vocal or physical expression, such as speaking, singing, shouting, clapping, dancing, etc. Praise also involves celebration. To praise God literally means "to boast" about God.

Try vocally and/or physically expressing praise to God today.

This exercise may feel new or out of your comfort zone. That's okay. I encourage you to give it a try and see what happens.

Following are a couple of ideas to help you get started:

1.   The Psalms are full of songs of praise to God. Pick a psalm of praise, such as Psalm 145, and read it out loud, vocally expressing praise to God from your heart.

2.   Pick one or two praise songs—upbeat music that gives praise to God. As the music is playing, try any or all of the following: sing, dance, clap, shout, jump, or anything else the Lord leads you to do. As you do these physical actions, let your heart express praise to God.

* * *

2 Chronicles 16:9 – *The eyes of the LORD run to and fro throughout the whole earth, to show Himself strong on behalf of those whose heart is loyal to Him.*

God is always looking for someone to partner with Him to release heaven's purposes on earth.

We can partner with God through faith and obedience in our daily lives. Whether it is obeying a prompting in our heart to make a phone call to someone, or picking up a flag and waving it during worship, God accomplishes heaven's supernatural purposes through us as we are obedient and submitted to Him.

Regarding the use of flags and other visual tools in worship, just as in anything else, we can act according to the flesh or according to the Spirit. For example, there may be two different people waving a flag. From the outward appearance, they both look like they are doing exactly the same thing. However, depending upon what is in their hearts, they may get different results. If we do something in the flesh, we will get flesh results. If we do something in the Spirit, we will get God's supernatural, life-giving results.

Galatians 6:8 (ESV) – *The one who sows to his own flesh will from the flesh reap corruption, but the one who sows to the Spirit will from the Spirit reap eternal life.*

In everything we do, the most important thing is what is in our hearts. God looks at our heart.

DAY 16

Activation:
Ask the Lord, "What is it that You want me to do today?"
Relax, take a deep breath, and listen to the still, small voice in
your heart. Purpose in your heart to partner with God in what
He wants to do through you today.

If you like, you can pray a prayer similar to this:
"Lord, I am a yielded vessel to You. I ask that You would
speak through me, move through me, and love through me
today. Make me an ambassador of Your love. I agree with You
and I want to partner with You in bringing forth heaven's
purposes on earth. I yield my heart to You. Thank You for
loving me. In Jesus' name, amen."

* * *

DAY 17

> 1 Samuel 16:7 – *The LORD does not see as man sees; for man looks at the outward appearance, but the LORD looks at the heart.*

Religion is concerned about our outward appearance and actions. However, God is interested in our heart, and that is what He is looking at. What is in our heart, and the motivation behind what we do, is more important than our actions or appearance. First Corinthians 13:1-3 describes this well:

> 1 Corinthians 13:1-3 – *Though I speak with the tongues of men and of angels, but have not love, I have become sounding brass or a clanging cymbal. And though I have the gift of prophecy, and understand all mysteries and all knowledge, and though I have all faith, so that I could remove mountains, but have not love, I am nothing. And though I bestow all my goods to feed the poor, and though I give my body to be burned, but have not love, it profits me nothing.*

For our actions to have any lasting value, our heart must be motivated by love. God is love, He is motivated by love, and as His children, we are reflections of who He is (1 John 4:8). Actions motivated by the love of God will bear godly fruit.

Activation:
Take some time to examine your own heart. Yield your heart to the God of love. Picture Him putting His heart into yours.

Use the following "**Heart Check List**" to examine your heart motives regarding any particular action. Ask yourself:

1. Why am I doing this?
2. Are my motives pure?
3. Is my motive the **love of God**?

Psalm 139:23-24 (ESV) – *Search me, O God, and know my heart! Try me and know my thoughts! And see if there be any grievous way in me, and lead me in the way everlasting!*

* * *

DAY 18

Proverbs 4:23 – *Keep your heart with all diligence, for out of it spring the issues of life.*

Proverb 4:23 highlights the importance of keeping watch over our heart. Every issue that manifests in our life has its root somewhere in our heart. What we believe in our heart determines the direction of our life.

Proverbs 23:7 - *For as he thinks in his heart, so is he.*

Our heart is like a gate. A gate is an entryway that can keep good things in and bad things out. It can also keep bad things in and good things out. We determine what we let into our heart, and what we keep out. We can choose to not let worldly influences into our heart and instead, choose to focus on what God's Word says. As we fill our hearts with God's way of thinking, our life will naturally bear God's kind of fruit, which is love, joy, peace, patience, kindness, goodness, faithfulness, gentleness, and self-control (Galatians 5:22-23). As long as we establish our heart in God's goodness and feed our heart with God's life-giving words and His love, our life will naturally bear godly and life-giving fruit.

Activation:
Take an inventory of your thoughts throughout the day and be aware of any thought that does not line up with the Word of God and the love of God. Be especially vigilant of what you see and hear on television, radio, or other media, as well as your own personal "self talk." Be conscious of what you are letting into your heart.

DAY 18

If something does not line up with the Word of God, you do *not* need to let it into your heart. If you see or hear something that does not line up with the Word of God or the goodness and love of God, you can simply say, "I don't receive that." Then speak the truth to your heart. This is one way to manage the gate of your heart to let the good things in and keep the bad things out (2 Corinthians 10:4-5).

* * *

DAY 19

Matthew 19:26 – *Jesus looked at them and said to them, "With men this is impossible, but with God all things are possible."*

Worship connects us into the realm of God. When we worship, we are actively engaged in God's Kingdom activity, and with God all things are possible.

Worship taps us into our spiritual power source, which is our intimacy with God. It is like an electrical plug getting plugged into an electrical outlet. Once plugged in, the power can flow through the cord to whatever appliance or device is attached to it, so that the appliance or device can effectively perform the job it was created to do. In worship, we consciously get connected with God, which facilitates His power flowing through us and into the lives and situations around us. What is impossible in the realm of man alone becomes possible through God's power flowing through us.

Activation:
Find a comfortable place to sit or lie down. Choose at least one or two worship songs that help you put your focus on the Lord. While the music is playing, close your eyes and picture yourself "plugging in" to your spiritual power source. Feel your heart connecting with God's heart. He is your life source. His life and power are flowing through you.

DAY 20

Proverbs 18:21 – *Death and life are in the power of the tongue, and those who love it will eat its fruit.*

In Genesis 1, we see that God created the world by speaking it into existence. Genesis 1:26 states that God created man in His image and likeness. Since we are created in God's image and likeness, our words also have creative energy. This energy can be either positive or negative. James 3 also describes the power of the tongue. Though the tongue is a small member of our body, it can literally change the direction of our life. If you are not totally satisfied with the current direction of your life, you can change it! Take an inventory of your words. We frame our world with our words.

How do we release life through our words? One way is by agreeing with what God says about us and about our situation. Worship is a place where we can meditate on God's promises in His Word, His love for us, and who we are in Christ. As these truths become real to our heart and we begin speaking it out, creative power is released to fulfill God's Word in our life.

Activation:
Choose a promise of God from His Word that provides the answer or solution to a current life situation. Speak this promise out loud several times during the day. As you speak the Word of God out loud, think about what you are saying and let it sink into your heart. Speaking the Word out loud helps establish the truth in your heart and releases life into your situation.

DAY 21

*Matthew 11:28 – Come to Me, all you who labor
and are heavy laden, and I will give you rest.*

In Matthew 11:28, Jesus gives us a special invitation. He
invites us to come to Him, and He will give us rest.

What is this rest? Rest has to do with ceasing from our self-
effort and trusting fully in Jesus' finished work. We do not
need to earn God's love and approval. He already loves us
completely and unconditionally (John 3:16, Romans 5:8,
Romans 8:38-39). We do not need to perform to determine our
value. God has already determined our value (Psalm 8:5). The
value of something is determined by what you are willing to
pay for it. The value He places on us is the value He places on
His dearly beloved Son (John 3:16).

God is inviting us to rest in His love and approval. He is
inviting us to trust Him as our source.

Jesus did the work so we could enter His rest. He lived a
perfect, sinless life, went to the cross, conquered the grave,
rose in victory, provided everything we need, and He is now
seated at the right hand of the Father—a place of rest—and we
are seated with Him (Ephesians 1:20). His rest has become our
rest. We receive it by faith and trust in Him.

Activation:
Psalm 23 is a beautiful picture of the rest God gives us as well
as a picture of total trust in Jesus, our Good Shepherd. Read
Psalm 23 slowly, verse by verse, out loud and let the words
paint a picture in your mind. Visualize yourself with the Good
Shepherd. Thank Him out loud after each verse, for His
goodness.

Psalm 1:1-3 – *Blessed is the man*
Who walks not in the counsel of the ungodly,
Nor stands in the path of sinners,
Nor sits in the seat of the scornful;

But his delight is in the law of the LORD,
And in His law he meditates day and night.

He shall be like a tree
Planted by the rivers of water,
That brings forth its fruit in its season,
Whose leaf also shall not wither;
And whatever he does shall prosper.

As we meditate on the words God speaks to us and set our focus upon Him, we tune ourselves into the presence of God. As we continue to do this, we become "planted" in His presence, "*like a tree planted by the rivers of water, that brings forth its fruit in its season, whose leaf also shall not wither; and whatever he does shall prosper.*" This is a picture of abiding in His presence, and drawing our strength and nourishment from His presence. Great fruit comes forth from abiding in the presence of God. His presence refreshes us and keeps us revitalized. As long as we continue to abide in His presence, the presence of God flowing through us causes us to prosper in everything we do.

Activation:
Take some time to focus on a Scripture verse that is meaningful to you or something the Lord has spoken to your heart. To "meditate" not only means to ponder, but also involves uttering or speaking out loud. Speak the word out loud as you ponder it. Continue speaking the Scripture verse or

word out loud as you visualize it becoming real in your life.

Continue to focus on the Lord until you feel yourself tuning into His presence. Picture yourself like the tree planted by the rivers of water, drawing your strength, nourishment, and refreshment from His presence.

* * *

Psalm 107:9 – *He satisfies the longing soul, and fills the hungry soul with goodness.*

God's presence is essential to life. Everything flows from His presence. He is the Author and Source of Life. God's presence is the answer to every need. The solution to every problem can be found in His presence.

So how do we make room for more of His presence? There is no limit or measure to what God can do. He has given us all of Himself. We can have and experience as much of God as we want. So the question is, how much of Him do we want? How hungry are we for God's presence?

Imagine you are planning to have dinner at a buffet restaurant. It is all-you-can-eat, so you want to get your money's worth! What would happen if you decided to eat a large snack right before going to the restaurant? You would probably not be able to eat very much when you got to the restaurant, because you were already full. On the other hand, those who go to the restaurant hungry would have room to eat more! Being hungry positions us to receive more.

Our hunger for God's presence will increase our capacity to experience more of His presence.

Activation:
One way to cultivate a hunger for more of God's presence is to place value on His presence. Whatever we value, we will make time for. Take an inventory of your time. What is your time being filled with? Are you setting aside regular time to spend with the Lord? Or are you getting full on other things? Ask the Lord to give you a greater hunger for His presence.

DAY 24

Revelation 22:1 – *He showed me a pure river of water of life, clear as crystal, proceeding from the throne of God and of the Lamb.*

In Scripture, water is often symbolic of the presence of God (Psalm 72:6, Hosea 6:3, Isaiah 44:3). What can we learn about the presence of God through this symbolism? First of all, water is essential to life—we cannot live without it. In the same way, the presence of God is essential—He is our source of life (Jeremiah 17:13). Secondly, water quenches thirst. The water of God's presence quenches our spiritual thirst (Psalm 42:1). Thirdly, water is refreshing. God's presence restores and refreshes us (Psalm 23:1-3). Fourthly, water cleanses and purifies. We are washed by the water of God's Word as we meditate upon His Word in His presence (Ephesians 5:26).

Revelation 22:1-2 describes the river of God's presence, flowing from His throne. It is a pure, refreshing, life-giving river. Hebrews 4:16 tells us that through Jesus, we can *"come boldly to the throne of grace, that we may obtain mercy and find grace to help in time of need."* We are invited to drink from the river of His presence.

Activation:
Find a comfortable place to lie down. Close your eyes and picture the river of life, flowing from the throne of God. It is the throne of His grace. Imagine yourself in the river of His presence, drinking from the river, and letting it wash over you. Feel the water of His presence refreshing you, cleansing you, and giving you life.

DAY 25

John 7:37-39 – *On the last day, that great day of the feast, Jesus stood and cried out, saying, "If anyone thirsts, let him come to Me and drink. He who believes in Me, as the Scripture has said, out of his heart will flow rivers of living water." But this He spoke concerning the Spirit, whom those believing in Him would receive; for the Holy Spirit was not yet given, because Jesus was not yet glorified.*

When we are filled with the presence of God, the by-product is that His presence will overflow to those around us. God's desire is for us to be filled with the fullness of His presence (Ephesians 3:19). When we are filled with God's presence, we do not have to "work at" ministering to others. Ministry will be a natural overflow of His presence from our lives.

God's presence in us is designed to affect those around us. Jesus describes the presence of the Holy Spirit in us as a river. A river is different from a lake, in that a lake is self-contained. In contrast, a river flows and brings life to everything around it. God's presence in us is designed to flow through us and bring life to the people and circumstances around us. His presence in us changes the atmosphere everywhere we go.

Activation:
Practice an awareness of God's presence throughout the day. One way to do this is to consciously thank Him throughout the day, even for little things. This trains our heart to look for God's presence. As we look for Him with expectation and gratitude, it opens our heart for God's presence to flow through us. An expectant heart is like a magnet for miracles.

Romans 14:17 – *The kingdom of God is not eating and drinking, but righteousness and peace and joy in the Holy Spirit.*

God's kingdom is a joyful kingdom. In fact, according to Romans 14:17, one third of the kingdom of God is described as joy! God created us to be filled with joy. Through the Holy Spirit, God put His joy in us.

Galatians 5:22-23 – *The fruit of the Spirit is love, **joy**, peace, longsuffering, kindness, goodness, faithfulness, gentleness, self-control.* [emphasis mine]

God desires us to experience joy abundantly in our daily lives. In John 16:24, Jesus states, *"Ask, and you will receive, that your joy may be full."* Jesus invites us into relationship with Him and gives us the privilege of praying to God the Father in His name and receiving the answers to our requests, so that we may be filled with His joy.

Just as it blesses a parent's heart to see his/her children happy and fulfilled, how much more does our Heavenly Father delight in seeing His children filled with joy? After all, the joy of the LORD is our strength (Nehemiah 8:10).

Activation:
Make time for joy. It's okay to give yourself permission to be childlike and have fun!

In Matthew 18:3, Jesus said, *"Assuredly, I say to you, unless you are converted and become as little children, you will by no means enter the kingdom of heaven."*

DAY 26

Plan some time today to do something you enjoy doing, and have fun with it! It doesn't have to be time-consuming or complicated. It can be as simple as putting on some music you like and dancing around the house for five minutes, while letting go of your cares and worries. Or it could be starting a project you've always wanted to try. Or calling a friend you haven't talked to for a while. Do something that makes you smile and brings joy to your heart.

Becoming childlike helps us find joy in simple pleasures. Give yourself permission to experience joy and have fun today! God delights in our joy!

* * *

DAY 27

Psalm 16:11 – In Your presence is fullness of joy; At Your right hand are pleasures forevermore.

Psalm 16:11 tells us that there is fullness of joy in God's presence. Contrary to how some have portrayed God, God is not angry or in a bad mood. One third of His Kingdom is described as joy, and God is full of joy! God is joyful, He is in a good mood, and He loves us! And when we spend time in His presence, and with others who also experience the joy of His presence, His joy tends to rub off on us!

There is complete joy in God's presence. In fact, God Himself rejoices over us:

Zephaniah 3:17 – The LORD your God in your midst, The Mighty One, will save; He will rejoice over you with gladness, He will quiet you with His love, He will rejoice over you with singing.

The Lord has joy and love in His heart when He looks upon us. He delights in us, and we bring Him joy.

Activation:
Sit or lie down in a comfortable, quiet place. Close your eyes and picture God rejoicing over you. He may be singing or dancing over you. He may look at you with His eyes filled with love and touch your face gently. Let Him quiet you with His love. Take a deep breath and feel His love for you. Feel the joy in His heart towards you. His heart is beating and brimming over with love for you. He has a big smile on His face and He is so delighted to be with you.

Philippians 4:4 – *Rejoice in the Lord always. Again I will say, rejoice!*

There is a difference between joy and happiness. Happiness is dependent upon circumstances or "happenings." For example, one tends to feel happy when something good happens. However, if something bad happens or there is disappointment, the feelings of happiness often go away. Joy is much more than a feeling of happiness. True joy is not dependent upon external circumstances.

In Philippians 4:4, the apostle Paul exhorts us to "Rejoice in the Lord always." To "rejoice" is an action verb. In other words, we have a choice to rejoice. We may not have a choice about our circumstances at the moment, but we always have a choice as to how we will respond. We can choose to become bitter or better. Just to clarify, God is a good God and He doesn't have any bad gifts to give. Troubles, hardships, and sickness are *not* gifts from God to make us better. However, God is able to redeem any situation and work good out of it (Romans 8:28). He is able to bring forth beauty from ashes (Isaiah 61:3).

Regardless of the circumstances, we can choose to thank God for His goodness and His ability to bring forth good out of any situation. We can thank Him that He has forgiven and redeemed us in Christ. We can choose to rejoice in Him. Today, let's make a choice to rejoice!

Activation:
One way to rejoice in the Lord is to give Him thanks. Say the following prayer out loud:

"Dear Lord, today I choose to rejoice in You. I thank You…"

Fill in the blank with at least ten things that you are thankful to God for. To help you get started, you may want to thank Him for who He is, and begin naming some of His attributes (e.g. "Thank You that You are love, Thank You that You are a good God, Thank You for Your wisdom, Thank You for Your forgiveness," etc.).

Feel your heart beginning to fill with joy as you purposefully thank God from your heart. As you practice this exercise, it will become easier and you may find that you want to keep on giving thanks. You may end up having a praise and rejoicing party with the Lord!

* * *

Proverbs 17:22 – *A merry heart does good, like medicine, but a broken spirit dries the bones.*

There are many benefits of living in joy. In fact, God has prescribed joy as part of our heavenly health care plan! Proverbs 17:22 tells us that a joyful heart does good like medicine. Laughter is healing. An added benefit is that joy does not have any negative side effects!

Another benefit of a joyful heart is that it helps us stay attuned to heaven's perspective. God is a joyful God who laughs at His enemies.

Psalm 2:4 – *He who sits in the heavens shall laugh; The Lord shall hold them in derision.*

If God laughs at His enemies and we are seated with Him in heavenly places in Christ (Ephesians 2:6), we too can laugh at our enemies.

Proverbs 15:15 – *All the days of the afflicted are evil, but he who is of a merry heart has a continual feast.*

God wants us to experience His joy on a continual basis. We do not have to let circumstances dominate our heart. Instead, we can choose to yield to the Spirit of joy, align ourselves with the God of joy, and enjoy a continual feast from the table of His promises.

Day 29

Activation:
Try laughing today! Do something that makes you smile and laugh. Or simply initiate laughter by saying, "Ha ha ha..." out loud. If there is a situation you are dealing with right now, you can bring it before the Lord and laugh over it by faith. Simply start saying, "Ha ha ha..." and begin declaring out loud promises of God that address your situation. You may feel a little silly doing this at first, but as you continue doing it ("ha ha ha...") it will help bring your mind into alignment with God's perspective. It reminds us of how big God is and how small our problem is compared with Him. Plus laughter increases oxygen flow to our body and reduces stress, which helps us feel better!

* * *

DAY 30

Psalm 37:4 – *Delight yourself also in the LORD, and He shall give you the desires of your heart.*

Worship is where we delight ourselves in the Lord. It is where we set our affections upon the Lover of our soul, gaze into His eyes of love, and experience His delight in us. He is so completely enamored with us, His Beloved, and His desire is for us (Song of Solomon 7:10).

Worship is a place of intimacy and delight. Worship is where we experience a unique and personal relationship with the One who knows and loves us intimately. Just as every marriage relationship is different, our relationship with the Lord is special and different from anyone else's. The Lord enjoys the uniqueness He created in each of us and we each fill a special place in His heart that only we can fill. As we experience oneness with the Lord in this place of intimacy, our heart becomes knit with His and He puts His desires in our heart. If we are intimately connecting with the Lord and delighting ourselves in Him, the desires in our heart will most likely be godly desires. And it is our Beloved's good pleasure to fulfill those desires.

Proverbs 13:12 (ESV) – *A desire fulfilled is a tree of life.*

Activation:
Take a moment to close your eyes and picture yourself with the Lover of your soul. He is smiling at you and He delights to be with you. Feel your heart connecting with His, and receive His love. Let your heart respond to His love.

DAY 31

1 Thessalonians 5:16-18 – *Rejoice always, pray without ceasing, in everything give thanks; for this is the will of God in Christ Jesus for you.*

One way to cultivate joy in our lives is through thanksgiving. Gratitude cultivates joy. As we practice being thankful and counting our blessings, it puts our focus on the goodness of God, and joy naturally begins to fill our hearts.

Throughout the Bible, we see God encouraging His people to remember and celebrate the things He has done for them. When we remind ourselves of what God has done for us, it helps establish His goodness in our hearts and strengthens our faith.

Giving thanks is a way of remembering what God has done. And remembering what God has done, in turn, inspires us to give thanks!

Sowing seeds of thankfulness yields a harvest of contentment and joy.

Activation:
Read Psalm 105. Notice how the psalmist begins by giving thanks and praise to the Lord, speaks of rejoicing, and then encourages the people to remember the wonderful things God has done for them. The rest of the psalm gives a detailed account of the great and mighty works of the Lord.

Initiate a flow of thanksgiving by writing your own psalm of thanksgiving to the Lord, remembering good things that God has done for you. Read the psalm out loud to Him.

Or simply write a list of things you are thankful to God for. It does not have to be elaborate. It can be as simple as thanking Him for the sunshine, or for providing food and shelter, or for a friendly smile. Try to write down at least twenty-five things that you are thankful for. Then thank God out loud for those things (e.g. "Thank You, Lord, for...).

Ultimately, we can cultivate joy in our hearts by thanking God on a regular basis and practicing a daily habit of thankfulness.

* * *

Proverbs 3:5-6 – *Trust in the LORD with all your heart, and lean not on your own understanding; in all your ways acknowledge Him, and He shall direct your paths.*

Proverbs 3:5-6 conveys a wonderful promise from God. As we put our trust in God and acknowledge Him, instead of trusting in ourselves, God promises to direct our steps.

One way of acknowledging God is by giving Him thanks. When we make a conscious effort to thank God, it opens our eyes to His goodness and faithfulness. When we see His goodness and faithfulness, it establishes His character in our hearts and builds our trust in Him. When we live from a place of complete trust in God's goodness and love, we can experience His peace and joy in any circumstance and know that He is directing our paths.

Giving thanks to God also helps establish His Word in our hearts. Thanking God for His promises is a way of meditating on the Word of God. It helps strengthen our faith and bring forth the manifestation of those promises in our lives.

Activation:
Choose a promise of God that is meaningful to you. Begin thanking God for that promise until it becomes real to your heart.

DAY 33

Isaiah 26:3 – You will keep him in perfect peace, whose mind is stayed on You, because he trusts in You.

How do we stay in perfect peace, regardless of the circumstances in our lives? The answer is found in Isaiah 26:3. The key to staying in peace is keeping our mind stayed on the Lord, and putting our complete trust in Him. In any circumstance, we can choose to put our eyes on the storm or put our eyes on the Lord (Matthew 14:28-33). Choosing to put our eyes on the Lord and trusting Him connects our heart to His heart and results in the fruit of peace in our lives.

One way to practice keeping our mind stayed on the Lord is through worship. In worship, we focus on the Lord and become immersed in His presence. The more often we enter into worship, the easier it becomes for us to tune into God's presence and keep our eyes on Him. As worship becomes a lifestyle, we yield our hearts to the Lord moment by moment and develop an awareness of His presence throughout the day.

Activation:
Find a comfortable place to sit or lie down. Choose at least two or three worship songs that help you put your focus on the Lord. While the music is playing, close your eyes and imagine yourself gazing upon the Lord. Take a deep breath, relax, and rest in His presence. Picture yourself bringing any worries or concerns to Him and putting them in His hands. Release your concerns to Him and purpose in your heart to trust Him. You will know that you have fully released your concerns to the Lord when you feel an inner peace in your heart.

Hebrews 12:1-2 – *Since we are surrounded by so great a cloud of witnesses, let us lay aside every weight, and the sin which so easily ensnares us, and let us run with endurance the race that is set before us, looking unto Jesus, the author and finisher of our faith.*

Have you ever noticed that you tend to move towards whatever direction you are looking? Whether driving or walking or dancing, our bodies tend to follow whatever direction our eyes are looking. Hebrews 12:2 exhorts us to look to Jesus, as we run the race set before us. As we journey through life, if we keep our eyes on Jesus, He will always lead us in the right direction.

Keeping our eyes on Jesus also helps us to walk in humility, because it takes our eyes off ourselves and fixes them on Jesus. Fixing our eyes on Jesus helps us to be less self-centered, which frees our heart to experience greater joy and freedom and also positions us to better perceive and receive what God is doing in our midst.

Activation:
Practice fixing your eyes on Jesus throughout the day today. Anytime you find yourself thinking about your problems or feeling inadequate or self-pity, just adjust your gaze: take your eyes off yourself and put them on Jesus. If this is a new exercise, it may take some practice at first, but don't be discouraged and don't beat yourself up! There is no condemnation in Christ Jesus (Romans 8:1). If you realize you took your eyes off Jesus, just lift your head up and put your eyes back on Him.

DAY 34

As you continue to practice fixing your eyes on Jesus, you will discover that your day tends to go much more smoothly when you keep your eyes on Him. You will most likely begin enjoying this exercise and wanting to practice it every day. Jesus will always lead you in the right direction!

* * *

Psalm 103:1-5 – *Bless the LORD, O my soul;*
And all that is within me, bless His holy name!
Bless the LORD, O my soul,
And forget not all His benefits:
Who forgives all your iniquities,
Who heals all your diseases,
Who redeems your life from destruction,
Who crowns you with lovingkindness and tender
mercies,
Who satisfies your mouth with good things,
So that your youth is renewed like the eagle's.

No matter how we are feeling at the moment, we always have a reason to rejoice and bless the Lord. In fact, Psalm 103 begins with a whole list of amazing benefits of being a child of God! He forgives all our sins, heals all our diseases, redeems us from destruction, crowns us with lovingkindness and tender mercies, satisfies us with good things, and renews our youth and strength! What an incredible benefits package! Psalm 68:19 tells us that God loads us with benefits every day:

Psalm 68:19 – *Blessed be the Lord, who daily loads*
us with benefits, the God of our salvation!

God does not hold back when it comes to blessing His children. He lavishes His love on us and *loads* us with benefits!

Activation:
Just as the psalmist did, we can choose to bless the Lord with everything that is in us, and remind ourselves of His benefits.

DAY 35

Read Psalm 103:1-5 out loud, consciously thinking about and connecting your heart with the words you are speaking.

Thank the Lord for daily loading us with His amazing benefits.

* * *

Day 36

> Isaiah 40:31 – *Those who wait on the LORD shall renew their strength; they shall mount up with wings like eagles, they shall run and not be weary, they shall walk and not faint.*

Are you feeling weary, tired, or weak? God promises to renew our strength as we wait on Him. To wait on the Lord does not imply sitting around idly. On the contrary, the word "wait" in the context of Isaiah 40:31 implies a focused looking, with expectancy. Picture a dog waiting expectantly for his master to come home. The dog may be looking intently out the window, or staying close to the door where his master could walk in at any moment. But his mind is completely focused on his master, looking to see him when he returns.

Here is another picture of actively waiting. Have you ever been to an upscale restaurant, where the waiter stands in the dining room with a cloth napkin draped over his arm, attentively watching the table he serves, to see if there is a need? The moment you take a sip of water, he comes quickly to refill your glass, because he is actively watching and waiting, ready to serve. He is immediately available when there is a need, because he has been watching with expectancy.

When we actively set our focus upon the Lord with expectancy, not only will He renew our strength; He will cause us to soar high above the circumstances and run with perseverance and joy the course He has set before us.

Activation:

Today, purpose in your heart to actively set your focus upon the Lord. Look intently around you to see how He is at work in your life and circumstances. Every time you recognize God at work, acknowledge Him by thanking Him for what He is doing. God is always at work. If you like, you can pray the following prayer:

"Dear Lord, thank You that You always desire to work good in my life. Open my eyes to see how You are at work in my life and circumstances, and help me to cooperate with what You are doing. Thank You for working good in my life, and that nothing is impossible with You. I love You, Lord, and I look forward to a great day together with You. In Jesus' name, amen."

* * *

Romans 8:6 – *To be carnally minded is death, but to be spiritually minded is life and peace.*

God has given us a recipe for life and peace in Romans 8:6. The fruit of being spiritually minded, or yielded to the Holy Spirit, is life and peace. Every day we have a choice to yield to the flesh, or yield to the Spirit of God. Every time we choose to yield to the Spirit of God, it produces life and peace.

The more time we spend with the Lord in His presence, the more spiritually minded we become. It then becomes easier, and even second nature, to yield to the Holy Spirit on a daily basis. As we delight in the goodness of God and receive His love for us personally, it feeds our spirit and we naturally want to do what gratifies the Holy Spirit. As a result, we experience more of His life and peace, and it becomes a lifestyle and cycle of blessing.

Activation:
Find a comfortable place to sit or lie down. Choose at least two or three worship songs that help you focus on the love and goodness of God. While the music is playing, close your eyes and feel your heart opening up and receiving the love of God.

If you have time, for additional meditation, read Romans 8. Focus on the love and goodness of God.

DAY 38

1 Corinthians 6:19 – Do you not know that your body is the temple of the Holy Spirit who is in you, whom you have from God, and you are not your own?

You are of great value to God. In fact, He chose you to be the temple, the very dwelling place, of His Spirit. Out of His great love for us, God sent His Son Jesus to pay the penalty for our sin, give us His righteousness in exchange as a gift, and restore us to intimate relationship with God. He gave us the gift of His Spirit to be our Comforter, Counselor, Helper, Intercessor, Advocate, Strengthener, and Standby (John 14:16, AMP). By placing His Spirit in us, we literally become joined as one spirit with God—this is a very intimate relationship!

Romans 8:11 – If the Spirit of Him who raised Jesus from the dead dwells in you, He who raised Christ from the dead will also give life to your mortal bodies through His Spirit who dwells in you.

The same Spirit who raised Jesus from the dead lives in us! God has given us access to His life and power—He placed it in us through His Spirit. We just need to draw upon the Holy Spirit and yield to Him, activating the power of God within us.

Activation:
Speak the following declarations based on Scripture out loud over yourself:

"God has given me the gift of His Spirit. My body is a temple of the Holy Spirit, who lives in me." (1 Corinthians 6:19)

"I am united to the Lord and am one spirit with Him."
(1 Corinthians 6:17)

"The same Spirit who raised Jesus Christ from the dead lives in me and gives life to my mortal body." (Romans 8:11)

* * *

DAY 39

3 John 1:2 – *Beloved, I pray that you may prosper in all things and be in health, just as your soul prospers.*

Just as it blesses a parent's heart to see his or her children prospering and content, God delights in the prosperity of His children.

Psalm 35:27 – *"Let the LORD be magnified, who has pleasure in the prosperity of His servant."*

God is a good Father and the giver of every good and perfect gift (James 1:17). It is His desire for His children to prosper in every area of life—spiritually, emotionally, mentally, financially, relationally, physically—you name it! In *all* things! And He has given us everything we need for life and godliness (2 Peter 1:3).

The source of our prosperity is our intimate relationship with Him. God is the One who gave us life, and He is our source of life. When we connect our heart with God's heart in worship, we are tapping into our life source, and His life begins to flow through us. As we connect intimately with God on a regular basis, He shares His heart with us, gives us wisdom and solutions to problems, and brings healing and the good gifts we need. As we renew our minds to our identity in Christ and begin to see ourselves as He sees us, we are empowered with boldness to walk forward in His destiny for our lives.

Activation:
Read Ephesians 1:17-23 and Ephesians 3:14-21 and pray both Scripture passages out loud as a prayer over yourself.

Daniel 11:32 – *The people who know their God shall be strong, and carry out great exploits.*

We need to be people who know our God, so we can be strong and carry out the great exploits He has called us to. Worship takes us deeper into the place of knowing and experiencing God. Our strength comes from our intimacy with Him. Our intimacy with God grows as we spend time in His presence. In worship, we immerse ourselves in His presence. We set our focus upon Him so that He is magnified above any problem or circumstance, and His solutions come into view.

In worship, we connect our hearts with God's heart and fine-tune our spiritual antennas to receive broadcasts from heaven. We receive wisdom and strategies from the Lord. In worship, God often reveals our assignments and imparts the grace, strength, and wisdom to fulfill them. In worship, God shares His heart with us, so that our hearts are moved with what moves His heart. Worship is where we connect with God so that we can do what we see our Heavenly Father doing (John 5:19). Worship is where we become like Him, for He is our Father, and we are His children, and *"as He is, so are we in this world"* (1 John 4:17).

Finally, worship is where we experience being His Beloved and let Him fill our hearts with His perfect love that casts out fear, so that we may boldly carry out His will, on earth as it is in heaven. God's love never fails! (1 John 4:18, 1 Corinthians 13:8)

DAY 40

Activation:
Sit in a quiet, comfortable place with a journal or notebook and a pen. Quiet your heart before the Lord. Picture Him smiling and delighting in you. Feel His love surrounding you. When you feel you are focused on His presence, write down the question, "Lord, what do you want to tell me right now?" Then relax and listen to the still, small voice in your heart and write down what you hear.

* * *

INVITATION PRAYER

If having an intimate relationship with God is a new concept to you, or if you have never invited Him to be the Lord of your life and you would like to begin this wonderful relationship with Him, He is waiting for you to come to Him with open arms!

You can receive God's personal invitation into an intimate relationship with Him by saying the following prayer, or a similar one, from your heart:

"Dear God, Thank You for creating me, loving me, and giving me life. Thank You for sending Your Son Jesus to pay the price for the wrong things I have done in my life and setting me free to be in relationship with You. Thank You for rescuing me and forgiving me. I now invite Jesus to be the Lord of my life. I invite Him to be my healer and my leader. I invite You to fill me with Your Holy Spirit. You have a home in my heart. Thank You for coming to live in me and to be with me forever. Thank You for the good plans You have for my life; I look forward to our adventures together. In Jesus' name, amen."

DEVOTIONAL NOTES

ABOUT THE AUTHOR

THERESA MURATA is the founder of Worship Expressions, a nonprofit organization dedicated to helping people experience worship, freedom, and healing through music, dance, and teaching the Word of God. She is a teacher, seminar speaker, and worship leader, as well as an author and recording artist.

Her passion is to see people healed and set free, and to bring people into intimate relationship with God.

Theresa earned a teaching degree from the University of Illinois and a ministerial diploma from Charis Bible College. She is a licensed and ordained minister.

AUTHOR CONTACT INFORMATION AND MINISTRY RESOURCES

Theresa Murata
Worship Expressions

worshipexpressionsmin@gmail.com
www.worshipexpressions.net

RESOURCES

Additional copies of this book are available at:

www.worshipexpressions.net
Amazon.com

OTHER RESOURCES BY THERESA MURATA

DANCING WITH SILKS: MOVING WITH THE WIND OF THE SPIRIT

Worship Dance Training Manual

"I highly recommend this manual! [Theresa's] spirit of excellence is displayed throughout her teaching!"
-Cindy Green, Minister of Dance

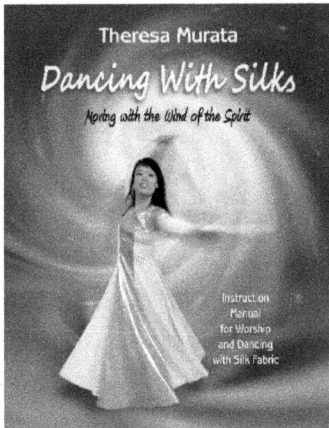

This manual is a tool for both teachers and students who desire to learn how to dance skillfully with silk material, as well as those who are seeking a deeper understanding of worship and the biblical use of symbolic tools, such as the silk, in praise, worship, and intercession.

Includes over 400 step-by-step photographs!

Available at:
www.worshipexpressions.net

OTHER RESOURCES BY THERESA MURATA

PEACE IN HIS PRESENCE

Instrumental Worship CD

PEACE IN HIS PRESENCE is a recording of original violin and keyboard music inspired by the Holy Spirit and the Scriptures. It is an invitation to enter deeper into God's presence and allow His peace to permeate your whole being. Experience waves of God's peace, love, joy, healing, and goodness wash over you as you rest in His presence.

Available at:
www.worshipexpressions.net
www.cdbaby.com
Amazon.com
iTunes

www.ingramcontent.com/pod-product-compliance
Lightning Source LLC
Chambersburg PA
CBHW060649030426
42337CB00017B/2514